Grandfather and Me

Merrilynn Wheeler

Grandfather and Me

An Angel's Kiss Poetry

Grandfather and Me
Copyright © 2011 by Merrilynn Wheeler. All rights reserved.

No part of this publication may be reproduced, stored in a retrieval system or transmitted in any way by any means, electronic, mechanical, photocopy, recording or otherwise without the prior permission of the author except as provided by USA copyright law.

The opinions expressed by the author are not necessarily those of Stonewall Press.

Published in the United States of America

ISBN: 978-1-64460-043-6 (*sc*)
       978-1-64460-042-9 (*e*)

Library of Congress Control Number: 2018963026

Published by Stonewall Press
4800 Hampden Lane, Suite 200, Bethesda, MD 20814 USA
1.888.334.0980 | www.stonewallpress.com

1. Family
2. Memoirs (Biography/Autobiography)

19.01.12

Also by Wheeler, Merrilynn

"I do Remember" Philadelphia Wedding Pages, Spring/Summer 1997

"You are Part of a Big Family" CHURCH EDUCATOR, January 1985

"Walking Two Moons in Another's Moccasins" CHURCH EDUCATOR, June 1985

"Don't Overlook the Small Things in Life" CHURCH EDUCATOR, October 1984

"A Youth Fellowship Overnight" CHURCH EDUCATOR, September 1985

"Vacation Bible School" CHURCH EDUCATOR, May 1984

"God's Circle of Love" CHURCH EDUCATOR, August 1983

GRANDFATHER and ME comes from a heart and mind that has thought in verse. My Grandfather never wrote a standard letter, he wrote in poetry. They say our talents come from past generations, I agree, for my ability to write in verse was handed down to me. My love for my Grandfather and Grandmother Hyde is kept alive in memories and reading his lines. He wrote to his sons at war; he wrote to his daughter and her family; he wrote to his granddaughters Donna and me.

I share these lines with you now in hope that you too will feel a moment of uplifting to the throne of God's love.

I dedicate this book of poetry to God and in honor of my Grandfather Hyde. It is God who gifts each one of us in ways that are meant to make this world a better place because He placed you and me in this moment of time.

Contents

AN ANGEL'S KISS Spirit Filled Poetry..................11

An Angel's Kiss..13
Blessed Assurances 15
Come In And Know Me....................................17
Deep Within The Heart Of God 19
Entertaining Guests..21
Everlasting 23
God's Instrument 25
God's Precious Earthly Gift–Mother 27
Heaven's Tears 31
Humility..33
I Am The Door 35
I Am Your Father 37
Morning Dove...39

DEAREST ONES   Life's Lessons 41

O Father God Hold Us In Your Embrace 9-11 43
Dearest Ones 47
Folks Like You 49
Is It Not Friendship..51
Today's Grief Cannot Hold 53
Wisdom...55

BIRTHDAYS Moments Of Joy 57

Birthdays 59
Fifty Years Of Bliss 61
My Precious One 63
My Treasure Lies With You 65
My Special "New Year's" Wish For You 67
Christmas Night Came Creeping 71
Santa Clause Land 73

AUNTI "TA DA" Laughter is Good for the Soul 75

Aunti "Ta Da" 77
City Farmer 79
Ludwig Von Ant 81
Playing Tag 85
The Joy Of A Merry-Go-Round 87

AN ANGEL'S KISS

Spirit Filled Poetry

An Angel's Kiss

Russell F. Hyde
(Intro lines written by Merrilynn Wheeler, 4-16-1997
upon finding the poem her Grandfather
wrote to her when she was 10 years old.)

"Grandfather—did an angel kiss you while you slumbered?"
The note I pinned to his shirt said
As he lay there napping on my bed.

To my surprise when I returned,
Upon my pillow, a note that read—

"My dear Granddaughter
An angel did kiss me last night
Although I was asleep
It made me dream you loved me so
I want that love to keep
It means so much for me to know
Of your devotion dear
It keeps your Grandpa young at heart
And fills my days with cheer."

Love from your devoted Grandfather

Blessed Assurances

Merrilynn Wheeler

"Blessed Assurance Jesus is mine…"
You need to feel it in your heart
To sing that line.
To know the pain of defeat, despair
And be lifted up from there,
To heights unknown and yet known.
To stand at the pinnacle and survey
The cathedrals you were placed within
To be a steward of the possessions
Of the King of Kings and Lord of Lords.
For you are of the Great, 'I AM"
Created by Him.

Come In And Know Me

Merrilynn Wheeler

Where is the sign that says—
'Come in and know Me better, child.'
What of coming in—where's the door
And knowledge—what for?

Why the strictness of acceptance
Was there a seating chart—
Weren't all, aren't all welcome to sup?
Why the barriers—whose afraid of whom?

With outstretched arms He bore it all
And
Brought salvation to the world.

Deep Within The Heart Of God

Merrilynn Wheeler

I sit deep within the heart of my Lord
Held fast and tight and buffered from sin
I know not what lies ahead or
If I can even win.

My questions increase as knowledge dims and I see
Within the mirror
That I am neither the beginning nor the end
But a part of the continuum of God's grace.

Oh I had thought the world
Was my oyster
And deserved the priceless pearl within
Until I came face to face with
The matchless grace
That brought me to my knees
Weeping in ecstasy that
He did not turn His
Face from me.
But lifted me into His embrace.

Entertaining Guests

Merrilynn Wheeler

Who's to say what angels do
Or how they come
Or what instrument they'll use?
Perhaps it is I or even you!

Who's to say when a stranger
Walks into your life
If you are entertaining a messenger of God?
But wouldn't wisdom say—
Act as though you are!

Everlasting
Merrilynn Wheeler

As you take the less traveled road
that leads beyond
the cradle,
the cross,
the grave
to life everlasting.

As you kneel in adoration at the manger crude,
lift your eyes and gaze upon
the Heavenly Realms,
the Throne of God,
the Sacrificial Lamb
that reigns at the right hand of God.

As you walk the twisting path of cobblestone
that leads to
the hill,
the tomb,
the garden,
Hear the angels' words, "He is not here."

As you breathe the sweet perfume of the lilies in the field,
gaze out upon
the moment,
the hour,
the day,
you find yourself walking close with Him
in His
EVERLASTING creation.

God's Instrument

Merrilynn Wheeler

I know of one who prays for thee
upon their knees
Who looks upon the Face of God
and cry's out,
"Why hast thou forsaken me…"
and then responds,
"Not My will God, but Thine be done."

I know of one whom, in her pain,
brought forth our Savior King.
Who held within her heart
All the joy and suffering.

I know of one who knows such separation
and yet finds solace in the
Arms Of God.
Who wandered about this world unwanted
and unloved.
Oh how I wish I could have been the mother
she needs,
As upon her knees, in the early morning,
before the altar of God,
She prays for me—

God's Blessings be upon this life—
For she has touched my heart
and I am strong in my resolve
that what I did, I did for Thee
As an instrument of the Family of God

Mom (Edith), George, & Merrilynn

God's Precious Earthly Gift—Mother

Merrilynn Wheeler

From time eternity God's plan for His creation
Is for His children
To know love unending;
To walk humbly before Him;
To show compassion and grace;
To "Honor your father and your mother,
As the Lord your God has commanded you,
so that you may live long and
that it may go well with you…" Deut. 5:16

For God provides for all our needs and calls us
To embrace the precious gift expressed
In the loving arms of mothers.
It is a calling that asks much
To selflessly be given,
To place another's life above their own
To take the child's hand and led them on their way;
To encourage and to pray,
To lift them up before the throne of God in response,

"Let the little children come to me, and do not hinder them,
for the kingdom of heaven belongs to such as these."

As years go by, life's challenges increase, and the value fades,
The gift appears old and out of touch,
God speaks
To the heart and mind of the child,
"Listen, my son, to your father's instruction
and do not forsake your mother's teaching." Prov. 1:8

For it was this Precious Earthly Gift
That knelt in ceaseless prayer.
Who from the moment you were placed within her life,
Sought out wisdom from above
To nurture, protect, guide, and love
As she answered her greatest calling
To be your mother.

Heaven's Tears

Merrilynn Wheeler

The still quiet music of Heaven's tears
Taps out a melodious tune,
That softens the rushing world.

If I could but compose this well
Choosing notes and beat
In sync with a higher realm.

To transport thoughts to loftier heights
One must listen long and well,
To the steadiness of tone,
To hear with soulful ears
And
Feel the heartfelt flow
Of spirit filled crescendos.

Humility

Merrilynn Wheeler

H =   Humbled before the throne of God
U =   Unable to speak for the very awe,
M =   Moved to great joy.
I =   I am but an image of Him,
L =   Loved so completely.
I =   I am the daughter—child of God
T =   Taken from the grip of sin
Y =   Yes wholly blessed and saved by Him.

I Am The Door

Russell F. Hyde

I Am the door my savior said
Thru Me, you'll find a peace
Thru Me, the joy of restfulness
You'll find will never cease.

If any man shall enter in
He surely will be saved.
Though he wear the cloak of faith
Or if he be depraved.

Many doors are opened wide
To let the crowds come in,
But they harbor deep regret
Because they lead to sin.

Enter through the Golden Door
Its portals are divine.
Your Savior will clasp you to His breast
And say, At last you are Mine.

I Am Your Father

Merrilynn Wheeler

My beloved daughter—
I am here as close to you as your breath, your thoughts
I am your Father—not your earthly one—
I am your Father
You belong to me and I love you My child—
Come to the mountaintop—
Dance with me—
See the light, feel the breeze, smell the fragrance—
You are mine, you are OK and you are my instrument,
I have much to do through you,
Your touch, your commitment.
I am your Father, God.

Morning Dove

Merrilynn Wheeler

Morning dove that coos so soft
The world does not hear nor embrace
The peace your song resounds.
For evil is rampant in the world
It blocks out grace and love
With the noisy clash of sin.

Respect wears no badge
It doesn't matter age.
Fifteen minutes of fame
Is now the game.
Is media to blame?

Where are the heroes and heroines
It use to be so clear,
The black hat meant bad,
The white meant good.

Then from the heavens realm
A cry—This is My Son
And He has died
You are set free, just believe,
Hold fast to right and good
And act accordingly!
Love your neighbor,
Stop the hate,
Stand firm,

Be a model not a mat.
Enter through the gate.
Be not afraid to speak and act
As Christ would do.
But first admit the grip of sin
Cannot be loosed without Him.
Know who you are.
A Child of God,
Who hears the still soft voice say—
'Come in and know you are saved'.

DEAREST ONES

Life's Lessons

O Father God
Hold Us In Your Embrace 9-11

Merrilynn Wheeler

I can look out upon Your creation
But those we lost cannot.
I can see the storm clouds forming
and wish upon the stars.
I can feel the rain drops falling
as I look up at the sky
and I can cry WHY?

I see Your tears Father
I hear your pain
as the thunder rolls
for so many of Your children
came home today.

Can there be a pain so great,
An ache so deep?
Let us not fail to respond in
love, truth and peace.

I see the leaves changing as
the earth prepares for sleep.
But oh how it must moan
as so many loved ones have gone home.

How have we failed to see that
life is so short,
How much we need to turn our thoughts
to the words that are Yours.

Oh Father-hold us in your embrace.

Show us that our acts must be mindful
that it might be our last.
What is so important Father but
our love for You.

May our hearts be changed towards others;
May this enormous loss not be in vain;
May it be a turning point.

Oh Father-such unspeakable pain.

Our eyes stay fixed upon the scene
In the periphery, our gaze is drawn
towards others who mourn.
Deep within Your heart Father
our loved ones have gone home,
no more to know this earthly pain.

America—GOD BLESS
One nation under YOU—

Oh my God, my Father
Help us in our all-consuming grief—
We each have been touched by this act of hate.
Father as we cry out,
change our words of revenge

to words of peace.
Let us not stoop to their level,
Let us not return evil for evil,
but as a phoenix-rise high
above the destruction
flooded with Your Grace.
A people who hold firm to what our fore-parents built,
A country built on Freedom
to speak, to write, to believe.

We stand stronger in our resolve
that no nation should feel such pain—
that Freedom must ring out upon all lands—
your children must know Your love
and we must lead the way.

Oh Father–give us the strength of resolve
and focused thoughts
and help us lead the way.

Dearest Ones

Merrilynn Wheeler

I basked in the expression of love of a
Universal family, unique in character,
Harmonious in nature.
Each person bringing to it their own specialties—
That I felt truly cared for and experienced a moment
of nurturing peace.
No greater gift could have been bestowed upon me,
Then to be shown there are those who wish to share
their lives with me.
Though our paths may part as years go by,
There is a bond that will ever hold us close,
For we are family in the eyes of God
And it has been made known within our hearts.

Thank you for the moments so richly blessed
By your love and tenderness.

Folks Like You

Russell Hyde

The shadows of the evening
Steals across the sky
I am sitting in my easy chair
And think of days gone by
I find it so relaxing
Each time I take a look
And read the many pages
In my memory book
Some were written many days ago
But the last ones are quite new
And tonight as I sit gazing
I am reminded Folks, of you
I don't know how it started
But the seed of Friendship grew
From the moment that I met you
I felt at ease and knew
That I was sharing something
Friendship brings to light
A Joy I often remember
When days have turned to night
I love to visit Folks Like You
The reason is to me
To step into your home and share
Your hospitality
These and many pleasantries
I have pondered in my mind

As I travel down my memory lane
Once more this joy to find
Yes, I love to visit Folks Like You
Because there is no fuss
And I am hoping someday soon
That you will visit us.

Merrilynn Wheeler

Is It Not Friendship

Merrilynn Wheeler

Life touches life,
Moment seizes moment,
Asking us to wait,
if only for a short while,
To realize that…

It is within the smile that we see the
joyful nature of the spirit.
It is within the gaze that we feel the
radiance of a heart.
It is within the words that we hear
the knowledge of the mind.
And, it is within the touch that we
know the compassion of the soul.

Is it not friendship that embraces
All this and more,
Transcending the limits of space and
time, holding each life gently in its'
embrace of memories.

Life is richer, fuller,
Because it seized a moment
To come to know you, my friend!

Today's Grief Cannot Hold

Merrilynn Wheeler

Today the grief seemed not so severe
As my ears did not hear the cries
Of the child my eyes would never see
Nor my arms ever hold.

How do you bury but a thought
There is no cemetery plot for empty tombs
Of unfulfilled life's dreams.

I would not have thought my heart would ache
For someone I had not thought of
Until it was too late.

Choices made some twenty years ago
Cannot be changed
But what did I know then
I did the most unselfish thing—
I raised another's child as my own.

Wisdom

Merrilynn Wheeler

The wise are not always the world's renowned
Philosopher or thinkers,
They're the ones who listen
To life's lessons,
Live life's lessons,
And pass those lessons on.

Thank you for reaching back and helping
Another on life's path.

BIRTHDAYS

Moments Of Joy

Birthdays

Russell F. Hyde
Written for a Birthday Party at the
Pensioner's Club in January 1959

Referring to Birthdays, we have only one.
But anniversaries, they surely do come.
When we were young, we could hardly wait,
For the coming of that desirable date.
With visions of presents, ice cream and cake
And the numbers of candles, the years indicate.
But when little girls reach close up to twenty,
They suddenly decide, this number is plenty.
So they say to the clock, "Let's start over again."
Until they are reaching three score and ten.
They then must admit they have now reached the age
When to be a golden Age'ers is now all the rage.
They have had their fun in hiding the truth
By living memory of their fast faded youth.
So they finally decided their age to admit,
Making it a secret didn't help, not a bit.
This also applies to most of the men
Who also have troubles with this three score and ten.
As powder and paint with them is taboo
They often will ask, "Just what can we do?"
Some get the answer, 'twas easy to find,
In reviving a hobby that was oft in their mind.
Some join a club, where Pensioners meet
And mingle with friends, a pleasure complete.

Russell Frederick Hyde and Amy Gibson Hyde

Fifty Years Of Bliss

Russell F. Hyde, May 1961

The wedding bells were ringing clear
In the 'fall' of long ago.
Me thinks I see two youngsters there
With romance all aglow.
Their hands and hearts were joined as one
as they stood before the Lord.
Now fifty years have passed with honor to their vows.
We come this day to ask for the blessings of the Lord
To keep their hearts and hands entwined as on their wedding day
Fifty Years Ago

My Precious One

by Russell Hyde, 1948

Valentine's Day is here again
I wonder how I knew
Is it because my precious one
Once more I think of you.
You do not need Dan Cupid's bow
To captivate my heart
Your sparkling eyes and happy smile
Subdued me from the start.
Although your only three years old
You make the joy bells ring
And at the end of tiring days
You cause my heart to sing!
So you see my lovely little one
I can't help loving you
On this day of Valentine
And all the others too.
You are the only little girl
That makes me always glad
That Cupid brought you here below
and made me your Grand Dad.

My Treasure Lies With You

Russell Hyde, 1949

I love you my darling every day
Of every month and year
Indeed each passing hour you have
Become more sweet and dear
But when the moment is at hand
For Valentine and such
My feeling of affection has
An extra special touch
You're my special interest
With all that love implies
You cause for me Romantic Stars
to illuminate my skies
I see a brighter sun by day
A softer moon by night
And in your own beloved eyes
There is a magic light
And so I say with sentiment
Forever old but new
That I adore you every Day
My treasure lies with you.

My Special "New Year's" Wish For You

Russell F. Hyde, 1953;
Featured in the Ridley Farms Chanticleer page 7
Update by Merrilynn Wheeler, March 19, 2010

This is my special New Year's wish for you.

When the New Year starts.
May there be sunshine in your heart
and your spirit gay,
As you start each new day.

May you be blessed with perfect health,
And be close to those you love most dear,
Throughout the days, the weeks, the months
Of this the coming year.

In every call by cell phone
And every email, face book, tweet, or blog new
May they bring encouragement
And happiness to you.

In every wish may peace and faith
Provide a melody
That will fill your days with hope
And purest ecstasy.

Without a disappointment and
Without a single tear,
And no unpleasant experience
To mar a perfect year.

A most delightful New Year
Is my heartfelt wish for you
Whatever else you wish for
May each one come true.

Christmas Night Came Creeping

Russell Hyde

When the night before Christmas
comes creeping around
You will be sleeping
not making a sound.
Santa will visit
with his bag full of toys
Some for the girls
and some for the boys
When you wake in the morning
you will get a big surprise
When you open up your gifts
and see with your eyes
You got what you asked
Dear Santa to bring
That he didn't forget
one single thing.
So three CHEERS for Santa
For mom and dad too
For making this Christmas
The best you ever had.

Santa Clause Land

Russell Hyde

'Twas the night
after Christmas in Santa Clause Land,
To rest from his labors St. Nicholas planned,
His reindeers were sheltered in their own private stalls,
He discharged all his helpers until early next fall,
The furry red coat was laid safely away,
With the boots and the cap, with its tassel gay,
Toasting his toes by a wood burning fire,
What more could a weary old Santa desire,
He settled himself by that comforting blaze,
And began to think of all those happy days,
Little children are pleased with the simplest of toys,
A doll for the girls, a drum for the boys,
"I've worked day and night for almost a year
To supply all the children I visit both far and near"
So he puffed on his pipe and remarked to his wife,
"Happy children is reward for my strenuous life,
From climbing down chimneys, my legs fairly ache
But it's well worth the trouble
for the dear children's sake
I would bruise every bone in my body to see
Those darlings' delight with gifts and a tree
With this comforting thought his face was a glow
As he looked thru the window
at the fast falling snow.

AUNTI "TA DA"

Laughter is Good for the Soul

Aunti "Ta Da"

Merrilynn Wheeler

Auntie Ta Da is my name!
Dreams are my favorite game!

Who are you?
What do you like to play?

You say it's Tom
and
Hockey is the game.

Oh, what fun!

But Tom, have you played it on the moon,
Or on the tip of a spoon?

Oh, Auntie Ta Da how silly you say.
How can I play on a spoon?

It's as easy as one, two, three!

Just close your eyes and make believe!

City Farmer

Russell F. Hyde, 1945

You've seen this before: "Have a Victory Garden—eat what you can, can what you can't"…Well here's a complaint from Russell Hyde of the Spinning Department:

>Now Victory Gardens are all the rage.
>Catalogues are scanned from page to page,
>I've just looked at mine, the pictures are grand.
>I feel I can do better by the twist of my hand.
>So with spade and a rake, I begin with a whim
>But soon I discover this thing is grim.
>I dig with the spade and I scratch with the rake.
>The next thing I know I'm beginning to ache.
>But I don't give up, keep digging of course
>Why, it's plenty of fun, like riding a horse.
>With plenty of work and plenty of sweat,
>Hey, this is the Spring I won't easily forget.
>Well, I quit for the day, put my tools in the cellar
>And wash up my hands like a happy young feller.
>The next morning comes without even a shirk,
>I've got to get up and go back to my work,
>As soon as my feet are touching the floor,
>I learn that my muscles are aching and sore.
>My arms are all sunburn; my back is all bent,
>My legs are all shaky; my strength is all spent,
>You can take it from me, I'll never wish harm
>To the fellow who likes to work on the farm.
>And now in the future, this is the score,
>I'm getting my greens from the grocery store.

Ludwig Von Ant

Merrilynn Wheeler

Once upon a time, I found myself in the middle of a dark green forest. There under the largest oak tree, from a hole, came the sweet sound of music floating up through the leaves. A light came from the hole and much to my surprise, as I looked down inside, I saw an ant sitting on a toadstool. He was playing a harp, keeping the beat with one leg and strumming the strings with the other five. The ant began to sing.

"I am Ludwig von Ant
good at Beethoven I'm not!
But Bach, Mozart and Handel of course
I'm as great as great can be!"

A chuckle came from my throat,
as the ant sang on with a chorus of glee!

"I may be little you see
But great music knows not
the size of me!"

BRAVO!!! I yelled.
Oh please come with me.
For I am Aunti "TA DA"
and your music I love!
You are wonderful
You are great
What a hit you would make.

Nearly frightened stiff,
he could hardly speak —
"Who is that up there?"

Why it is me, Aunti "TA DA"
Please come up so we can meet.

My excitement increased with each step he took,
getting closer and closer to me.

Ludwig von Ant, May I call you Lu?
How do you do?

"I am fine thank you much.
Now please tell me just why you are here
and what it is you want with me!"

Oh LU how the children would love you.
What a thrill it would be
for them to see
you playing the harp and keeping beat with your feet,
Would you come to the Note Academy with me?

"The Note Academy?
Yes, I've heard of the Academy.
How excellent it would be to go to such a place.
How honored I am you picked me.
When do we leave?"

We'll leave right now if you please.

"My harp is all I need.
I'm as ready as I'll ever be."

So from the dark green forest, came Aunti "TA DA" with
Ludwig von Ant on her shoulder strumming
his harp and singing with glee.

"I'm Ludwig von Ant
good at Beethoven I'm not
but at Bach, Mozart and Handel of course
I'm as great as great can be
For now I'm off to the Note Academy."

Playing Tag

Merrilynn Wheeler

It was a strange and wonderful sight
It was big,
It was bright,
It was out of sight.
Just as fast as it appeared,
It disappeared.
Oh how I wish I could see it again,
All fluffy and white, floating in the air.
No strings to hold it there.
It was free to be!

It's fun playing tag,
Just the clouds and me.

The Joy Of A Merry-Go-Round

Russell Frederick Hyde, June 15, 1946
and Merrilynn Wheeler, March 19, 2010

There's a carnival in town,
Oh please, I want to go.
I remember Grandpa telling me
That he went when he was a boy.

He said, "The carnival was big and loud,
With all kinds of sounds.
But the one that caused a thrill in me was from the
Merry-go-Round!"

"When it came to a stop,
Without a thought,
I jumped up on a big gray Mare
And yelled, 'Getty Up HORSE!'
It wasn't going fast enough
So I tried a little force.
This just wouldn't do,
So I quickly switched
To the BIG BLACK STALLION
of course.

It was a thrill, I can't explain
As the Merry-go-Round went faster,
and the Stallion leaped higher.
It caused me to forget the time
I was having so much fun.

I held on tight and stretched my arm
To grab the BIG BRASS RING
I tried my very best at every turn
it meant one more ride that's free!

Granddaughter, you may not believe it
But before my ride was thru
I finally got that BIG BRASS RING
And next round I got TWO!
I'll say I got excited,
I stayed right on the horse's back
And took another spin,
BUT
all too soon that STALLION
Stopped dead in his tracks
My rides were through!

But when they open up again
You know just what your Grandpa did?
Why I got back up on that
BLACK HORSE
and grabbed a
BIG BRASS RING,
why, I grabbed TWO!"

www.ingramcontent.com/pod-product-compliance
Lightning Source LLC
Chambersburg PA
CBHW052112070526
44584CB00017B/2445